Dedicated to anyone who was told to toughen up and that big kids don't cry.

I feel this, I feel that, I feel emotions, how about that.
I feel red, I feel blue, sometimes green, how about you?

I feel happy, yes I do.
I feel happy, I know it's true.

I feel mad, yes I do.
I am mad, what do I do?

I feel sad, sad I am.

Do you feel sad? Tears are not bad.

I feel scared, scared I am.

Do you feel scared? I know I am.

I feel confused, yes I do.

What does that mean? Are you confused too?

I feel safe, yes I do.

My space is safe with me and you.

I feel tired, tired I am.

Do you feel tired? Sleep is the plan.

I feel grateful, grateful I am.

Do you feel grateful? Can you tell me then?

I feel love, yes I do.

Do you feel love between me and you?

I feel this, I feel that, I feel emotions, how about that.
I feel red, I feel blue, sometimes green, how about you?

But wait, we're not done, it's time to have more fun!

Colours make us feel things we can't utter,
colours make our hearts flutter!

Before you reach the end, let's start over again.
Pick a colour on the page, how does that make you feel?

Sometimes up and sometimes down,
emotions are like a ferris wheel.

Purple, green, red and blue just to name a few.
The colours of the rainbow all begin within you.

What did you discover about how you feel from colour?